D1131847

Reptile World

Green Iguanas

by Vanessa Black

Bullfrog Books

Ideas for Parents and Teachers

Bullfrog Books let children practice reading informational text at the earliest reading levels. Repetition, familiar words, and photo labels support early readers.

Before Reading

- Discuss the cover photo. What does it tell them?

- Look at the picture glossary together. Read and discuss the words.

Read the Book

- "Walk" through the book and look at the photos. Let the child ask questions. Point out the photo labels.

- Read the book to the child, or have him or her read independently.

After Reading

- Prompt the child to think more. Ask: Have you ever seen a green iguana? Was it wild or a pet?

Bullfrog Books are published by Jump!
5357 Penn Avenue South
Minneapolis, MN 55419
www.jumplibrary.com

Library of Congress Cataloging-in-Publication Data

Names: Black, Vanessa, author.
Title: Green Iguanas / by Vanessa Black.
Other titles: Bullfrog books. Reptile world.
Description: Minneapolis, MN: Bullfrog Books, [2017]
Series: Reptile world
Audience: Ages 5–8. | Audience: K to grade 3.
Includes index.
Identifiers: LCCN 2016002941
ISBN 9781620313831 (hardcover: alk. paper)
Subjects: LCSH: Green iguana—Juvenile literature.
Classification: LCC QL666.L25 B53 2017
DDC 597.95/42—dc23
LC record available at http://lccn.loc.gov/2016002941

Editor: Jenny Fretland VanVoorst
Series Designer: Ellen Huber
Book Designer: Lindaanne Donohoe
Photo Researcher: Lindaanne Donohoe

Photo Credits: Alamy, 14–15; Biosphoto, 13, 16; Dreamstime, 10–11, 23tl, 24; Getty, cover; iStock, 3, 23tr; Shutterstock, 1, 4, 5, 8–9, 12, 22, 23bl; ThinkStock, 6–7, 17, 18–19, 20–21, 23br.

Printed in the United States of America at Corporate Graphics in North Mankato, Minnesota.

Table of Contents

A Long Jumper 4

Parts of a Green Iguana 22

Picture Glossary 23

Index 24

To Learn More 24

A Long Jumper

What is in the tree?

It's a green iguana!

He is a big lizard.
How big can he grow?
More than six feet
(1.8 meters) long!

He lives in the rain forest canopy.

He eats leaves.

He eats fruit.

He basks in the sun.

Iguanas see very well.
What does he see?

It's a snake!

The iguana puts up
his spines.

It makes him look bigger.

Some animals would go away.

Not this snake!

She comes closer.

The iguana runs to the end of the branch.

He jumps.

17

Splash!

He lands in the river.

His long tail swishes.

His body moves side to side.

What a good swimmer!

Parts of a Green Iguana

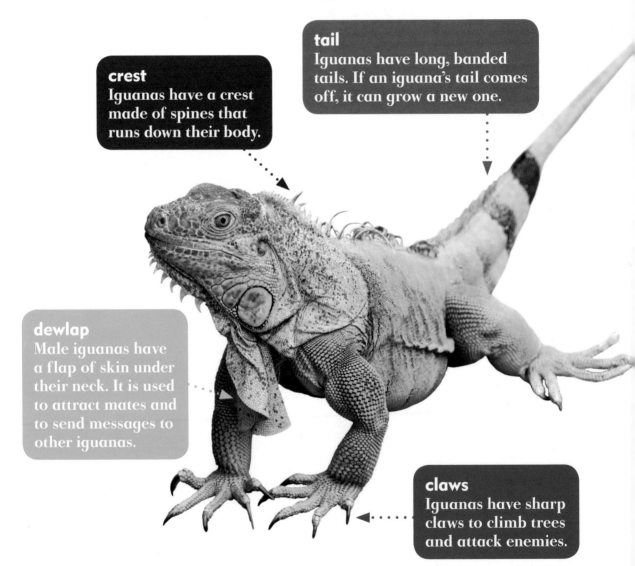

crest
Iguanas have a crest made of spines that runs down their body.

tail
Iguanas have long, banded tails. If an iguana's tail comes off, it can grow a new one.

dewlap
Male iguanas have a flap of skin under their neck. It is used to attract mates and to send messages to other iguanas.

claws
Iguanas have sharp claws to climb trees and attack enemies.

Picture Glossary

bask
To lay in the sun.

lizard
A kind of reptile with a long tail and four legs.

canopy
The place where branches and leaves of trees overlap.

swish
To move back and forth.

Index

branch 17

canopy 8

fruit 8

leaves 8

lizard 7

rain forest 8

river 19

snake 13, 16

spines 14

sun 11

tail 20

tree 4

To Learn More

Learning more is as easy as 1, 2, 3.

1) Go to www.factsurfer.com

2) Enter "greeniguanas" into the search box.

3) Click the "Surf" button to see a list of websites.

With factsurfer.com, finding more information is just a click away.